THE BAPTISM IN THE HOLY SPIRIT

The Baptism in the Holy Spirit: Why It's For Today and Why It Matters

Copyright © 2020 by Brian Connolly

All rights reserved solely by the author. The author guarantees all contents are original and do not infringe upon the legal rights of any other person or work. No part of this book may be reproduced in any form without the permission of the author. The views expressed in this book are not necessarily those of the publisher.

Scripture quotations taken from the New American Standard Bible® (NASB), Copyright © 1960, 1962, 1963, 1968, 1971, 1972, 1973, 1975, 1977, 1995 by The Lockman Foundation Used by permission. www.Lockman.org

ISBN-13: 9798631093447

A Publication of Tall Pine Books
|| tallpinebooks.com

THE BAPTISM IN THE HOLY SPIRIT

Why It's For Today and Why It Matters

BRIAN CONNOLLY

Tall Pine

This book is dedicated to my four daughters, Emma, Lily, Hannah, and Shiloh. It's my sincere desire that you experience and walk in the things written about in this book. I want nothing more than for my life's experiences to be yours and for you to love God with all that you are. May you fulfill the reason for which you were created. May you seek Him and find Him. And may your life be filled with God encounters. I love you girls so much and your dad is proud of you!

This book is also dedicated to every hungry and thirsty Christian that knows deep within their heart that something is missing in their life. May your hunger and thirst be satisfied as you read this book. May your search for more be quenched and may you find answers to the questions you've been longing to have answered.

ACKNOWLEDGMENTS

To Nicole — I couldn't ask for a greater wife! You've proven to be my greatest cheerleader, my best friend, and the one who has believed in me the most. Thank you for your love, your support, and for the sacrifices you have made for the ministry. I couldn't do what I do without you. You're the best and I love you so much. There is no one else I'd rather do life with!

To Adam — You are the closest friend I've ever had. I can't believe we get to do ministry together! Apart from Nicole, no one has cheered me on as much as you. You are always quick to rejoice with me and you always challenge me to use my gifts and talents to the fullest. You're an incredible leader and its my joy to submit to your leadership. Thank you for being open to the baptism in the Holy Spirit all of those years ago.

To Praise Community Church — You guys are my family. I'm exceedingly grateful for a group of people who love me and my family the way you do. Thank you for trusting me, for believing in me, and for sowing into my itinerant ministry. I love you all so very much.

To Will — Thank you for laying hands on me the night of December 3, 2009. That moment has forever changed my life. I'm grateful to have done life with you for as long as I was able. Thank you for giving me opportunity after opportunity to travel with you and minister alongside of you. Those moments taught me more than you'll ever know.

To Dan — Thank you for helping to shape much of the revelation contained in this book. You are one of the greatest teachers and examples in the body of Christ that I know. Your example and friendship has ministered to me in more ways than I could ever express. Thank you.

To Steve and Kelly — Thank you for standing alongside me and my family during one of the most trying seasons in our lives. Your love and support during that time was salve in the midst of all of the rejection we faced over this topic. I honor you for that. Thank you for believing me and for not thinking I was crazy. Thank you for continuing to stand with us after all of these years. We love you so much and are so grateful for your constant friendship.

CONTENTS

A Note from the Author	xiii
Introduction	xv
1. The Three Baptisms	1
2. Born Again By vs. Baptized In the Holy Spirit	9
3. God Never Changes	17
4. What's the Purpose of this Baptism?	27
5. What Happens When You Receive this Baptism?	35
6. Personal Testimonies	53
7. Healing Japan	79
8. How Can I Receive the Baptism in the Holy Spirit?	93
9. Prayer of Impartation	101
About the Author	103

A NOTE FROM THE AUTHOR

If you're anything like me, you've often felt like something was missing from your Christian experience. You may not have been able to put your finger on it, but you know deep down within yourself that there has to be more than what you are currently walking in. This is why I have written this book.

I've written it for people like you and for people like me to show you that you're not alone and that you're not crazy. What you have been sensing is right and it's from the Lord. Through your wondering and curiosity, He's been wooing you into an encounter with Himself that will forever change your life. I believe that the book you hold in your hands could be the very instrument that God uses to lead you into that encounter.

As you read, expect to feel stirred. Expect to feel excited. Expect your hunger for God to increase. And expect your heart to race at the possibility of experiencing what's described within these pages.

Whenever such moments occur, be sure to stop and soak in what's happening. Talk to God about what you're experiencing and ask Him to make such things a reality in your own life. Invite Him to immerse you into His very presence.

If you do this, if you're attentive to every nudge of the Spirit along the way, I truly believe you will encounter the blessed experience of being baptized in the Holy Spirit, or, at the very least, become so hungry for it that you will not stop seeking Him until He fills you with the promise of Himself.

INTRODUCTION

For the past few years, I have felt that one aspect of my calling from the Lord was this: to reintroduce the person of the Holy Spirit to the church. There is so much controversy and discrepancy when it comes to the person and doctrine of the baptism in the Holy Spirit.

In fact, I have personally experienced more backlash and persecution within the church over this one topic alone than over any other. It's my desire to present both sound, biblical teaching alongside of compelling, first hand testimonies involving this blessed experience to illustrate to and help convince the reader that Jesus is the baptizer in the Holy Spirit and that He is still doing it today.

I am exceedingly convinced that the enemy has worked hard to veil the truth of this experience through false doctrines and arguments and divisions within the body of Christ. It is, in my opinion, one of the greatest and necessary facets of the Christian life and God is wanting to reintroduce it to the church. It is the *greatest* and the *one* doctrine, in my opinion, that needs to find its way back into the pulpit and into Christian experience.

And I believe it's urgent.

One of the greatest tragedies when approaching the bible is that we have a tendency to read what we believe rather than allowing what we read to shape what we believe. In other words, we often read scripture through a lens. This lens is usually composed of what we've been taught by those we admire and by what we have or haven't experienced. My prayer for you, dear reader, is that you'd approach this book with a desire to understand the truth and that no matter what you've been taught or told about this subject, you would ask the Lord to help you approach what you are about to read without bias.

In fact, I'd encourage you to grab your bible and search these things out yourself while reading. You'll come across a great many scriptures and I challenge you to open the word of God yourself and see if what you are reading in this book is indeed the truth. And as you do, please come with an open mind. Come with sincerity of heart. Come with a desire to understand. If you do, I believe you will in fact experience the purpose for which this book is written and the experience it details.

1
THE THREE BAPTISMS

THE BAPTISM OF THE HOLY SPIRIT

One day while listening to a sermon on YouTube, I heard a well known, Texas preacher say that a Christian should ultimately experience three baptisms in their life as a new creation. The first one is that which is wrought by the Holy Spirit. It is what is commonly referred to as 'the new birth' or 'the born again experience.'

In his first letter to the church at Corinth, Paul helps us to understand this first baptism by writing, "For by one Spirit we were all baptized into one body, whether Jews or Greeks, whether slaves or free, and we were all made to drink of one Spirit" (1 Corinthians 12:13). The body that the Holy Spirit baptizes us into is the body of Christ. It's in that very moment that we become both the children of God and a new creation (see 2 Corinthians 5:17).

Jesus further explains this phenomenon to a man by the name of Nicodemus. Our Lord tells this inquisitive Pharisee that unless he is born again, he cannot see the kingdom of God. Perplexed by this statement, Nicodemus wonders how this could be possible since a man is incapable of reentering his mother's womb to be born a second time. Jesus reveals this mystery by explaining, "...unless one is born of water and the Spirit he cannot enter into the kingdom of God. That which is born of the flesh is flesh, and that which is born of the Spirit is spirit" (John 3:5-6).

In other words, it's the Holy Spirit that causes us to be born again. In the twinkling of an eye, He baptizes us into the life that is Jesus Himself (see John 1:4). In a moment, we are completely regenerated and renewed (see Titus 3:5). In essence, we become brand new. We receive a new nature and we are sealed in Christ by the Holy Spirit (see Ephesians 1:13).

THE BAPTISM OF THE DISCIPLES

As born again Christians, we have a mandate from the

risen Lord to make disciples of all nations (see Matthew 28:19). This commission was the final command that Jesus gave to His followers before ascending to the right hand of His Father in heaven. Attached to this commission is the directive to baptize new converts in the name of the Father and the Son and the Holy Spirit. But by what means is this baptism performed? What exactly are these new believers being baptized into?

Water.

In fact, this may be a good place to define what the word baptism actually means. In the original Greek language that the New Testament was written in, the word 'baptizō' is defined as the following in Strong's Concordance: to immerse, submerge, to overwhelm, to dip repeatedly. To be baptized into something is close to the equivalent of walking out into the ocean and being overcome by a wave of salty water. You'd no longer be the same. You'd be wet from head to toe.

That is exactly what happens whenever you are baptized into something. You're changed in an instant and you carry along with you the evidence of what it is you were immersed in. If you are baptized into Christ by the Holy Spirit, you become a new creation. Your desires change. The way you think changes. Your language changes. And you can no longer enjoy the sin you used to indulge in. You get a brand new heart.

This baptism into a new life by which we die to sin and are now alive to Christ is symbolized through water baptism and it is carried out by Jesus' disciples. Water baptism is a type of death and resurrection. Through it, we go down into the water, which is symbolic of the grave, and we rise up out of it, which is a symbolic representation of being born again or resurrection.

In Romans 6:3-4, Paul says it best when he writes the following:

> "Or do you not know that all of us who have been baptized into Christ Jesus have been baptized into His death? Therefore we have been buried with Him through baptism into death, so that as Christ was raised from the dead through the glory of the Father, so we too might walk in newness of life."

Through water baptism, we symbolically follow the example of our Lord and Savior. It's the outward manifestation of an inward reality. Through it, we are declaring that we understand that we are dead to sin — it is no longer our master — and are now alive in and through Jesus. We are also stating that we are no longer living for ourselves, but for the One who gave His life as a ransom for many.

THE BAPTISM OF JESUS

While John the Baptist was busy preparing the way of the Lord by urging his fellow Israelites to repent and be baptized for the forgiveness of their sins in the Jordan River, he took the opportunity to address a group of Pharisees and Sadducees. Through his exhortation, he plainly distinguished his ministry from the ministry of the One who would be coming after him through one notable difference. John declared, "As for me, I baptize you with water for repentance, but He who is coming after me is mightier than I, and I am not fit to remove His sandals; He will baptize you with the Holy Spirit and fire" (Matthew 3:11).

In other words, Jesus is the baptizer in the Holy Spirit. This is His ministry. He is the One who immerses you into the third member of the Godhead. To be baptized in the Holy Spirit is to be baptized into God Himself. Doesn't this sound like an intense experience? If you were baptized with the Holy Spirit and fire, don't you think you would know when that precisely happened?

Through this baptism, the Holy Spirit comes upon you and empowers you to be a witness for the Lord (see Acts

1:8). We will say more about this empowerment in detail in a later section. We will also discuss what else happens in the life of the individual as a result of receiving this experience at a later time.

It's important to note that the baptism in the Holy Spirit is discussed in every gospel. The reason why this is significant is because there are very few moments in Jesus' life that are recorded in each gospel. Matthew, Mark, and Luke are called synoptic gospels. They are similar in presentation and content. John, on the other hand, is not a synoptic gospel. However, these four things are unequivocally written about in each gospel: the death, burial, and resurrection of Christ and the baptism in the Holy Spirit.

THE THREE BAPTISMS IN THE OLD TESTAMENT

In 1 Corinthians 10:1-2, Paul writes:

> "For I do not want you to be unaware, brethren, that our fathers were all under the cloud and all passed through the sea; and all were baptized into Moses in the cloud and in the sea..."

Moses is a type of Jesus. He was raised up by God to deliver the Israelites out of Egyptian bondage. Their deliverance out of slavery is symbolic of being born again and where sin is no longer master over us. The sea that collapsed upon the Israelite pursuers, the Egyptians, is representative of water baptism. It washed away their captivity along with their captors in the same way that water baptism is symbolic of our freedom from sin and a life united to both the death and resurrection of Jesus. The cloud is the very presence or Spirit of God. It was with the Israelite's during their pilgrimage in the wilderness and it led and guided them.

The Israelite's baptism into these three things foreshadows the baptisms in the New Covenant that we've already discussed. They point to something greater that can now be experienced by every born again believer because of the death and resurrection of Jesus Christ. But how do you know if you've received this baptism?

What's the evidence?

When does it happen?

What's the purpose?

How can a person receive it if they haven't already?

I will do my very best to answer those questions and more throughout the remainder of this little book.

CONCLUSION

To be baptized into something is to be both immersed in and to carry along with you the evidence of your submersion. To be baptized is to be changed. When you're baptized into Christ, you become a new creation. When you are baptized in water, you become wet. And when you're baptized in the Holy Spirit and fire, you receive what the remainder of this little book will discuss in the chapters to come. Before we do that, however, let's further distinguish the difference between being born again by the Spirit and being baptized in the Holy Spirit.

2

BORN AGAIN BY VS. BAPTIZED IN THE HOLY SPIRIT

A WELL SPRINGING UP

IN JOHN 4, WE READ THIS VERY UNIQUE, RELATABLE STORY that I believe embodies what life is like apart from a relationship with Jesus. Wearied from His journey, Jesus decides to rest against a well. It's here that people would come to draw water to drink and to quench their thirst. And it's here, at Jacob's well, that Jesus has a conversation with a woman who has been looking her entire life for what He freely offers.

This is evidenced by the fact that this woman has had five husbands and the man she is currently with is not her spouse. Every man was a well of water. After they could no longer satisfy her thirst, she moved on to the next one. Such is life when Jesus doesn't quench our thirst for love, purpose, significance, acceptance, joy, and peace. We will drink from whatever we can in hopes to find what only He can give. This is what makes Jesus' interaction with this woman so relatable.

In an effort to get straight to the point and her very heart, Jesus asks this woman for a drink. While caught off guard and all but scoffing, she responds by pointing out that He is a Jew and that she is a Samaritan. In other words, they shouldn't be having this conversation since neither group has dealings with one another.

Jesus goes on to say, "If you knew the gift of God, and who it is who says to you, 'Give Me a drink,' you would have asked Him, and He would have given you living water" (John 4:10). The woman quickly points out that He doesn't have anything to draw out the contents within the well and that the well is deep. She, while playing into Jesus' hands, curiously asks the following question: "Where do you get that living water?"

Knowing that He has her right where He wants her, Jesus drops this incredible truth:

> "Everyone who drinks of this water will thirst again; but whoever drinks of the water that I will give him shall never thirst; but the water that I will

give him will become in him a well of water springing up to eternal life." (John 4:13-14)

This is the born again experience.

In 1 Corinthians 12:13, Paul says that we were all made to drink of one Spirit. It's this drink that becomes a well of water springing up to eternal life within a person. After listening to the gospel and receiving it by faith, the grace of the Lord, by the Holy Spirit, causes the hearer to become born again. Once this takes place, the person becomes the sole inheritor of an imperishable inheritance reserved for them in heaven (see 1 Peter 1:3-4). That inheritance is an eternity lived in the very presence of God and the promise of a dwelling place within the Father's house (see John 14:2).

In that same moment, the person also becomes a brand new creation where ALL things become new (see 2 Corinthians 5:17). Everything about them changes. Whereas they were once fathered by lies and possessed a nature of sin, they immediately become children of God born of Christ's seed (see 1 John 3:1 and 1 Peter 1:23) and they receive a new, heavenly Father.

RIVERS FLOWING OUT

It's important to note that when we drink from the offer

of the promise of eternal life, it becomes a well of water that springs up from within. This particular role of the Holy Spirit that causes us to be born again is significant because it is separate from another role of the Spirit that Jesus highlights later in John's gospel. The difference is contained in the symbolic representation of water.

Showcasing and helping us to see this difference, John, by the Holy Spirit, writes the following words:

> "Now on the last day, the great *day* of the feast, Jesus stood and cried out, saying, 'If anyone is thirsty, let him come to Me and drink. He who believes in Me, as the Scripture said, 'From his innermost being will flow rivers of living water.'' But this He spoke of the Spirit, whom those who believed in Him were to receive; for the Spirit was not yet *given*, because Jesus was not yet glorified." (John 7:37-39)

A well springing up is different from rivers that flow out.

To be born again by the Spirit is different from being baptized in the Spirit.

Notice, however, that both actions are the byproduct of a drink and the byproduct of coming to Jesus. Only God can take something so small and cause it to become larger than life. One drink becomes a well and leads to eternal life. Another drink becomes a river and causes us to become effective witnesses.

A well springing up is for my sake, but rivers that flow out is for your sake. One is between me and God. The other is so that others may experience God through me. It's in that moment that the river flowing from my innermost being becomes a drink for someone else to experience that may become a well inside of them. It's the manifestation of God in our lives through the Holy Spirit that invites others to become thirsty for what He offers.

RECEIVE, BUT WAIT

In an effort to further distinguish being born again by the Spirit from being baptized in the Spirit, let's look at a dialogue that Jesus has with His disciples shortly after He's raised from the dead. In John 20:21-22, Jesus tells His disciples that He is sending them in the same way the Father sent Him. In other words, His mission is about to become their mission. The torch is being passed from teacher to student.

He then does something that is loaded with spiritual significance. He breathes on His disciples and says,

"Receive the Holy Spirit." Why is this so compelling? Jesus does for His disciples what God did for Adam. After God formed Adam from the dust of the ground, He breathed the breath of life into his nostrils and man became a living being (see Genesis 2:7). Adam was born by the breath of God and we are born again by that same breath. And this breath is the Spirit Himself.

When Jesus breathed on His disciples, this was the moment that they were born again. They were recreated. They were made new. They came alive within and received a new nature.

The reason why this is so important is because shortly after Jesus breathes on them and says, "Receive the Holy Spirit," He tells them to wait in Jerusalem until they receive what the Father had promised — that they would indeed be baptized with the Holy Spirit (see Acts 1:4-5). Now, why would He tell them to wait when it already seems as though they received the Holy Spirit? He tells them to wait because being born again by the Spirit and being baptized with the Holy Spirit are two distinct and separate experiences. The words of Jesus in Luke 24:49 also serve to reinforce this point.

> "And behold, I am sending forth the promise of My Father upon you; but you are to stay in the city until you are clothed with power from on high."

Now that we've come to understand that these two experiences are indeed unique from one another, let us seek to answer the following questions: When and how is someone baptized in the Holy Spirit and does it still happen today?

3
GOD NEVER CHANGES

JESUS THE BAPTIZER

ONE THING IS FOR CERTAIN: JESUS IS THE SAME YESTERDAY and today and forever (see Hebrews 13:8). Although a seemingly small verse, it packs one heck of a punch, nonetheless. It's a verse we must wrestle with and pay attention to. It is, in my opinion, one of the greatest arguments supporting whether or not the baptism in the Holy Spirit is for today.

It's significant because Matthew 3:11 plainly states that it is Jesus that baptizes us with the Holy Spirit. Now, following the logic that Jesus is the same yesterday, today, and forever, we must infer that He is then still baptizing people with the Spirit today and will continue to tomorrow. If He never changes, His ministry never changes. This sentiment is also supported through key verses in the book of Acts.

THE LAST DAYS

When the day of Pentecost finally arrived, the Holy Spirit was poured out upon the waiting disciples. Faithfully obeying Jesus' command to wait until they received what was promised to them by the Father, these followers of our Lord were suddenly endowed with supernatural power and began speaking in languages they were never taught. All who were gathered that day began hearing the disciples glorify God in their native tongue (see Acts 2:1-11).

Not understanding what was taking place, the onlookers supposed that the disciples were drunk. Peter, full of the Holy Spirit, stood and with a loud voice explained to his audience that which was written by the prophet Joel was now being fulfilled.

> "'And it shall be in the last days,' God says, 'That I will pour forth of My Spirit on all mankind; and your sons and your daughters shall prophesy, and your young men shall see visions, and your old men shall dream dreams...'"(Acts 2:17)

The last days describes the time period we are currently living in. It's the period between Jesus' ascension to the Father and His return. It's during this interim period when God promises to pour out His Spirit on all mankind or on all flesh. It's important to stress that ALL means ALL! It includes men and women, young and old. This verse wasn't just limited to the people that were present during the delivery of Peter's emboldened message. This promise is for every person — those that were alive then, those that are alive now, and those who have yet to be born.

In fact, Peter goes on to say to those who were pierced to the heart by his sermon while being made aware that they played a part in Jesus' crucifixion that if they repented and were baptized, they would receive the gift of the Holy Spirit (see Acts 2:37-38). The gift of the Spirit that Peter was referring to is the baptism in the Holy Spirit. Concerning this, he also goes on to say the following in verse 39: "For the promise is for you and your children and for all who are far off, as many as the Lord our God will call to Himself."

Who could Peter possibly be referring to? Who are those that would fit the description of being 'far off?' It's us! He's referring to those who were to be born at a later time! The baptism in the Holy Spirit is not limited to a specific era of time. It's a ministry that is still being performed by the One who never changes!

WHEN AND HOW DOES IT HAPPEN?

More often than not, the baptism in the Holy Spirit is a subsequent experience. Although a person can receive it at the time when they are born again, this is exceedingly rare. There is only one place in scripture that details such an occasion. Let's look at several examples throughout the book of Acts that illustrate that being filled with the Spirit is something that follows the experience of being born again. We'll also examine the one place where a person can be born again and baptized in the Spirit at the same time.

SUBSEQUENT EXPERIENCES

ACTS 2 AND 4

We've already taken note of the fact that the outpouring of God's Spirit upon the disciples on the day of Pentecost was an experience that followed shortly after their born again experience when Jesus breathed upon them. They received it while waiting on God in prayer. This is one of the ways this particular baptism is received. They knew it was something promised to them and their faith in this promise caused them to wait upon it until it was received.

Shortly thereafter, this same bunch is filled with the Spirit again after they ask for greater boldness to speak the word of God with confidence (see Acts 4:29-31). Here again, we see that this is an experience that accompanies prayer. This particular instance also tells me that being filled or baptized in the Spirit isn't necessarily a one time occurrence. It is something we can continuously receive as we continue to humble ourselves before the Lord and ask for it. It also tells me that there are greater degrees of the baptism in the Holy Spirit and that we should continue to seek them out.

ACTS 8

The following is written after the ministry of Philip reaches the region of Samaria:

> "Now when the apostles in Jerusalem heard that Samaria had received the word of God, they sent them Peter and John, who came down and prayed for them that they might receive the Holy Spirit. For He had not yet fallen upon any of them; they had simply been baptized in the name of the Lord Jesus. Then they *began* laying their hands on them, and they were receiving the Holy Spirit." (Acts 8:14-17)

Samaria received the word of God through Philip. In other words, they were born again. This is further evidenced by the fact that they were baptized in the name of the Lord Jesus. Again, this is what disciples do. They baptize new converts in water in the name of the Lord.

However, the Holy Spirit had not yet fallen on any of them. Isn't that interesting? They were born again, but they weren't baptized in the Holy Spirit. Because the promise of this experience for these new believers was so important, Peter and John were sent to them. They traveled nearly 40 miles from Jerusalem to Samaria. That's a long ways to go! They didn't get in the car and do 65mph. They would have traveled on foot or by horse or by donkey. This distance and time it would have taken to travel illustrates how important it is to the apostles that these new believers receive this baptism.

It's important to note through this example that this baptism is not just received through waiting on God in prayer. It's also bestowed through the laying on of hands by those who have already received it; in this case, Peter and John.

ACTS 10

This is the only biblical account where people are being saved and baptized in the Holy Spirit at the same time.

While Peter was sharing the good news with Cornelius and Cornelius' relatives and good friends, the Holy Spirit fell upon those who were listening (see v. 44). Although rare, this particular instance does help us to see that it is indeed possible to be born again and filled with the Holy Spirit at the same time. Through this example, God was declaring that Gentiles (non-Jews) were now able to receive the gospel and the gift of the Holy Spirit.

It also goes to show that the baptism in the Holy Spirit can precede water baptism! At the very least, this story helps us to see the importance of not placing God in a box or reducing Him and His ways to a formula or method. Just when you think you have Him figured out and that you can anticipate what He's about to do, He tends to employ a different strategy to get the same result and do something we did not expect!

ACTS 19

While Paul was in Ephesus, he happened upon a group of 12 disciples who were only familiar with John's baptism — a baptism that involved submersion in water for the repentance of sins, a baptism that prepared a person to receive the good news of Jesus Christ. He asked them this very key question: "Did you receive the Holy Spirit when you believed?" (see v. 2).

Their answer to this question is stunning and I believe it would sadly resonate with the majority of the church today. Indeed, their response is synonymous with what I believe would be the response of many church goers.

They replied, "No, we have not even heard whether there is a Holy Spirit." The church at large tends to be more familiar with the Father, the Son, and the holy scriptures. Sadly, there is very little talk today about the person of the Holy Spirit. When we neglect Him, we neglect God because He *is* God. Not only that, He is the only member of the Godhead on the earth today! He is also the only member of the Godhead that we can grieve (see Ephesians 4:30). We grieve Him when we neglect Him and when we, as a result of unbelief, do not allow Him to do through us what He once did through Jesus. We must learn how to honor and cherish Him.

Paul knew how important it was that these 12 people receive the gift of the Holy Spirit. This is evidenced in the fact that his question is the first thing he says to these disciples when he stumbles upon them. Of all the questions he could have asked, he asked if they received the Holy Spirit!

After Paul explained that John prepared the way for Jesus, they were then baptized in the name of the Lord.

Following their profession of faith in Christ, Paul laid his hands on them and they were then baptized in the Holy Spirit.

> "And when Paul had laid his hands upon them, the Holy Spirit came on them, and they *began* speaking with tongues and prophesying." (Acts 19:6)

Paul's encounter with these 12 people once again illustrates that the baptism in the Holy Spirit can be received through the laying on of hands.

CONCLUSION

If Jesus is the same yesterday, today, and forever, and if He is the one who baptizes with the Holy Spirit and fire, then Jesus is still baptizing people with this baptism today. Scripture supports the fact that this baptism is received by either waiting on God in prayer or through the laying on of hands by those who have already received this baptism. Although it is often a subsequent experience to being born again, it is possible to receive it at the moment of salvation. In the next section, we will examine what the purpose of this baptism is.

4
WHAT'S THE PURPOSE OF THIS BAPTISM?

POWER

THE PRIMARY PURPOSE OF THE BAPTISM IN THE HOLY Spirit is to receive power to be a witness for Jesus. Without this baptism, our witness is rendered ineffective and is reduced to the fuel of our own efforts and human wisdom at best. The problem with this approach is that what we tend to do in the flesh we have to maintain in the flesh. Although our efforts may be sincere, they lack the power and ability to bring genuine transformation and awareness of the person of Jesus.

So many services within the church tend to revolve around entertainment and not the presence of God. We don't need better smoke machines, higher quality lighting, or tighter moments in worship. Don't get me wrong. I'm not opposed to excellence. But we can have all of those things and not have Him. We can have the form of godliness and not God Himself.

How tragic.

It's God that we need. We need His power so that people's faith doesn't rest in men, but in God, and it's found in the baptism of the Holy Spirit. This is what Jesus had to say about the purpose of this baptism:

> "...but you will receive power when the Holy Spirit has come upon you; and you shall be My witnesses both in Jerusalem, and in all Judea and Samaria, and even to the remotest part of the earth." (Acts 1:8)

This baptism took a group of 120 cowering men and women and turned them into a bunch of fearless, bold, miracle working disciples! It caused Peter, who, moments before, felt totally disqualified by his three denials to preach the boldest sermon ever recorded on the day the Spirit was poured out. It empowered Stephen and others to courageously make a defense for the gospel before a group of religious leaders and suffer death and great persecutions. And it resulted in Paul evangelizing the greater part of Asia Minor.

The power that accompanies the baptism in the Holy Spirit is the enablement to live and demonstrate the Christian life by the Holy Spirit. All of Christ's followers are commanded to follow Him. This is impossible without receiving the very power that operated in and through Jesus. Acts 10:38 reveals what rested upon and manifested through the Son of God.

> *"You know of* Jesus of Nazareth, how God anointed Him with the Holy Spirit and with power, and *how* He went about doing good and healing all who were oppressed by the devil, for God was with Him." (Acts 10:38)

Jesus did no ministry of any kind until He was baptized in the Holy Spirit Himself (see Matthew 3:16). It was the anointing of the Spirit that granted Him the power to heal the sick, raise the dead, cast out demons, and cleanse lepers. It is impossible to follow in His steps without being clothed with the same power. Not to mention, if Jesus needed to be baptized in the Holy Spirit, how much more do we need to be?

This empowerment in the life of the early church granted Jesus' disciples the ability to function in the gifts of the Spirit like speaking in unknown and known tongues and prophecy. It resulted in great courage in both speech and conduct when they were persecuted, which fulfilled what Jesus said when He told His followers to not worry about what they would say when they were handed over to the courts, for it would be the Holy Spirit who would speak through them (see Matthew 10:19-20). Signs and wonders also flourished at the hands of the apostles and their preaching was emboldened. Their understanding of the Scriptures greatly increased and they began to be led by the Spirit as well.

The following is a detailed compilation of the many wonderful things Jesus' followers did in the book of Acts as a result of this glorious baptism:

- A gathering of about 120 people began speaking with other tongues (Acts 2:4).
- Peter preached a sermon that pierced the hearts of the hearers and resulted in 3,000 people getting saved (Acts 2:14-41).
- Peter and John healed a lame beggar (Acts 3:1-8).
- Peter and John proclaimed Christ to those who were seeking to stop their ministry through intimidation (Acts 4:5-12).
- Many signs and wonders were happening through the apostles (Acts 5:12).

- The sick in the streets were being healed as Peter's shadow passed over them (Acts 5:14-15).
- Those afflicted with unclean spirits were being healed (Acts 5:16).
- Some apostles defended the ministry they were called to obey before the threats of the Council and high priest (Acts 5:27-32).
- Stephen performed signs and wonders among the people (Acts 6:8).
- Stephen proclaimed the testimony of God and His Christ to a group of religious leaders and asked for their forgiveness while being stoned to death (Acts 7).
- Philip preached Jesus in Samaria and performed many signs (Acts 8:5-8).
- Philip is led by the Spirit to preach Jesus to an Ethiopian (Acts 8:29).
- Paul begins to preach Christ shortly after being converted and baptized in the Spirit (Acts 9:20).
- Peter heals a man who had been bedridden for eight years (Acts 9:32-34).
- Peter raised a woman named Tabitha from the dead (Acts 9:36-41).
- The Holy Spirit sends Peter to preach the gospel to Cornelius and his household resulting in the Gentiles hearing the good news

for the first time and receiving the Holy Spirit (Acts 10:19-48).
- Paul takes the eyesight of Elymas the magician who opposed their ministry (Acts 13:9-11).
- Paul discerned that a lame man had faith to be made well and commanded him to stand up. He was immediately healed (Acts 14:8-10).
- Paul cast a spirit of divination out of a slave-girl (Acts 16:16-18).
- Paul and Silas sang hymns and praises to God after being beaten and imprisoned. Their example led to the salvation of their jailer and his house (Acts 16:23-32).
- The handkerchiefs and aprons that Paul touched were given to the sick and they were healed and evil spirits came out (Acts 19:11-12).
- Paul raised a young boy named Eutychus who fell out of a third floor window from the dead (Acts 20:17).
- Paul heals a man with recurrent fever and dysentery (Acts 28:8).

CONCLUSION

Indeed, receiving power to perform signs and wonders through the Holy Spirit is a key aspect of being a witness for Jesus. Paul claimed to have fully preached the gospel of Christ through his own testimony and signs and wonders through the power of the Spirit (see Romans 15:18-19). The gospel isn't adequately nor fully shared unless a demonstration follows it. Signs and wonders are the means by which the gospel is demonstrated. And the truth is that a person cannot be a witness for Jesus without receiving the very anointing that rested upon the One they are called to follow.

It's this power that causes men and women to operate in the gifts of the Spirit, heal the sick, cast out demons, raise the dead, and cleanse lepers. It grants them boldness to preach the gospel and to face persecution with courage. It amplifies the voice of God and allows them to be led by the Spirit of Jesus.

In the next section, we will examine what happens when you receive this baptism. I will draw upon both scripture and my own personal experience to help you better understand what the result is when a person is filled or anointed with the Holy Spirit.

5
WHAT HAPPENS WHEN YOU RECEIVE THIS BAPTISM?

MY STORY

IT WAS THE EVENING OF DECEMBER 3, 2009. IT WAS THE second day of a four day conference that I was attending in Mechanicsburg, PA. The speaker on stage was sharing about his personal experiences in ministry and the various times he and others were baptized in the Holy Spirit. The message was titled "How Thirsty Are You?" I remember sitting in my chair and thinking to myself, "It's all real. I want what this man is talking about. I want more of God. I need what this man has. I need to be filled with the Holy Spirit."

The primary reason I was attending this particular conference was due to the fact that I had been battling a

20-year-addiction to pornography and I had wanted to be delivered from it. I had done everything in my natural strength to rid myself of that bondage, but it was to no avail. The conference name contained the word 'deliverance' and that was all I needed to know to justify the purchase of my ticket and to solidify my attendance. God had set me free of multiple forms of drug addiction and a three year, carton-a-week cigarette habit through an encounter with His salvation at 19 years of age. If He could do that, surely He could set me free of my addiction to pornography.

After the minister was finished his message, he informed all of us what was about to take place. He said he was going to invite the Holy Spirit to come — it's not that the Holy Spirit wasn't already present, for there is nowhere we can go to escape the presence of God (see Psalm 139:7), but there is a difference when He manifests in the room. The minister then said that some of us may experience different phenomena in our bodies as the Holy Spirit began manifesting.

Heat.

A tingling sensation in our extremities — much like when your arm or leg falls asleep.

A current flowing through our bodies similar to that of electricity.

A cold sensation.

A weight pressing down on our shoulders.

Peace.

Crying.

Laughing.

Trembling.

The minister simply explained that these are some of the manifestations that he has seen when doing meetings like this and that they are signs that the Holy Spirit is touching an individual. I'd encourage you, dear reader, to not get caught up in these things and allow them to bring into question the truth that Jesus is still baptizing people in the Holy Spirit today. The truth of the matter is that we shouldn't be surprised that an individual would have such experiences if the Holy Spirit — the very power and presence of God on earth — is touching them. Surely the human body would respond to such an experience with an all powerful God!

Sadly, people often get hung up on the whole 'falling down' thing. When King Solomon dedicated the temple to the Lord, the 120 people who were gathered that day could not stand to minister (see 2 Chronicles 5:11-14).

Now we, through the New Covenant, are the temple of the Holy Spirit (see 1 Corinthians 6:19). Why is it so hard to believe that when He fills a person, they may not be able to stand? At the same time, not everyone falls! One experience isn't greater than the other.

We must learn to stop criticizing and judging what we don't understand or what we ourselves haven't experienced. Rather, we must learn to weigh it. We must examine the fruit of the experience. If a person is genuinely transformed by the experience and is more in love with God and people than they were before the encounter, then we must conclude that it was of God. The enemy of our soul would never do something that would cause such a result. He isn't trying to foster intimacy with God. Rather, he's seeking to destroy it.

No sooner did the minister utter the words, "Holy Spirit, come," I immediately found myself riddled with some of the symptoms he mentioned could befall us. I felt like I was being pushed over from behind. This is the glory of God. The glory of God is the weightiness of God. I saw and felt my hands tremble and felt heat in them as well. In fact, I remember that they became sweaty, too.

The minister continued to invite the presence of the Holy Spirit for a few more minutes before calling those of us who were experiencing Him down to the front. I was the first one there. I found myself just a few feet away from the stairs of the platform before one of the other ministers of the conference came down, laid his hands on my face, and said one word that has forever changed my life, "Fill."

Immediately, I collapsed to the ground. I had zero control of my legs. They were no longer capable of supporting my own weight, let alone the weight of what just came upon me. My hands curled up against my chest as I laid face down on the carpet. I then began shaking violently on the floor and my breathing quickened in rhythm with the power that was manifesting on my body. On top of this, I began crying. I cried as He healed emotional wounds in my life. And I cried over the fact that God was exceedingly real and that He was touching me.

I'm not sure how long this experience lasted, but I do know one thing: it marked me and forever changed me. Never have I ever experienced anything like that in all my life. My 20-year-addiction to pornography was instantly broken. It has now been 10 years since I last looked at a pornographic image. Not only that, I have zero desire to do so. That's how you know you're truly set free. You no longer think about what you were once enslaved to!

FREEDOM

Friends, I'm here to tell you that what Jesus did by the Spirit, the baptism in the Holy Spirit can also perform. Through the anointing of the Holy Spirit, Jesus healed all who were oppressed by the devil (see Acts 10:38). In an instant, I learned the meaning of the following words contained in Zechariah 4:6: "Not by might nor by power, but by My Spirit." The strength of flesh will never set you free of a spiritual issue. I desperately needed the power of God to set me free of the immorality that bound me. When Jesus filled me with the Holy Spirit, it instantly displaced whatever else was occupying what He wanted to fill. Pornography didn't stand a chance against the power of God!

LOVE

Aside from being completely and totally delivered from pornography, the other immediate change I noted was the love that flooded my heart for God. Romans 5:5 tells us that the love of God is poured into our hearts by the Holy Spirit. This, my friends, is what I believe to be *THE* evidence for being filled with the Holy Spirit. For the first time in my life, I felt like I could love God the way I've always wanted.

He was constantly on my mind. My thoughts would drift to Him often. Memories of that sweet experience between He and I filled my soul. All I wanted to do was be in His presence. My prayer life changed dramatically after that encounter. I would continuously prostrate myself before Him for hours as I filled whatever room I was in with worship music. I couldn't get enough.

Not to mention, I also found myself more readily able and willing to obey Him. I was passionate about praying for others and fulfilling the call of God on my life. It is, after all, those that obey Him that love Him (see John 14:21). Obedience is the love language of the Lord.

GOD REALITY

The experience of being baptized in the Holy Spirit brought a whole new dimension of the reality of God into my life. Although I knew He was real prior to this moment, this encounter served to both solidify and intensify that knowledge. He became more real than ever. John 15:26 says, "When the Helper comes, whom I will send to you from the Father, *that is* the Spirit of truth who proceeds from the Father, He will testify about Me." This is exactly what happened to me. Through this experience, the Holy Spirit revealed Jesus to me in such a way that He became exceedingly personal. There was no way anyone could have talked me out of what had happened to me, and believe me... they tried.

BOLDNESS

The way I ministered from that day forward forever changed. I wanted EVERYONE to experience what I had experienced. I began praying for the students that I led as a youth pastor to be filled with the Holy Spirit and they were having dramatic encounters! The only problem was that their parents didn't know how to relate to their child's experiences. In just a few short months, rumors had spread that I was under demonic influence and that I was a false prophet, a wolf in sheep's clothing.

On many occasions, both at the first church I served and at other places where I've ministered, I've had people confront me, question me, and seek to get me to stop through the use of intimidation. Unfortunately for them, it hasn't worked. I will not back off from what I know is true and I would do everything I've done all over again. That's how important it is to me that others encounter God and that He'd become real to them. Prior to being filled with the Holy Spirit, I would have bowed to their disagreements and intimidation.

We read about this kind of boldness that's the byproduct of being filled with the Spirit in Acts 4:29-31. Shortly after Peter and John were arrested, questioned by the religious leaders and released, the disciples prayed for greater courage to do the very thing that just got them in trouble!

> "And now, Lord, take note of their threats, and grant that Your bond-servants may speak Your word with all confidence, while You extend Your hand to heal, and signs and wonders take place through the name of Your holy servant Jesus." And when they had prayed, the place where they had gathered together was shaken, and they were all filled with the Holy Spirit and *began* to speak the word of God with boldness."

POWER

The first miracle that I bore witness to after being baptized in the Holy Spirit was the disappearance of a brain tumor. One of my wife's co-workers had a son who was diagnosed with said tumor. This concerned mother invited me and my wife over to pray. We laid our hands on this teenage boy and commanded the tumor to go in Jesus' name. He has been tumor free ever since!

I also noticed a greater authority and power in my preaching. I would often step back in myself while speaking and think, "This is not the same Brian!" I had more confidence. I had a greater assurance. And I felt more alive when I did it. I knew this is what I was called to do.

I also began to see demons manifest and cast out. One particular man was delivered from a spirit of rage shortly after I was filled with the spirit. A teenage girl was delivered from a spirit of fear. And a dear friend of mine was delivered from a spirit of suicide and depression.

Again, Acts 1:8 tells us that it's this kind of power that is the byproduct of the baptism in the Holy Spirit that grants us the ability to be witnesses for Christ.

HEARING GOD'S VOICE AND PROPHECY

Hebrews 4:12 tells us that the word of God is alive and active. No truer words were spoken when I began reading my bible after I was baptized in the Holy Spirit. Something glorious happens when the author of the scriptures fills you. He helped me to understand them. This is exactly what happened to Peter on the day of Pentecost. He was immediately able to discern by the Spirit that what was happening was prophesied in Joel 2:28-29 (see Acts 2:16-21). Likewise, Stephen was able to preach Jesus from the Old Testament scriptures, beginning with Abraham, to the religious leaders who questioned him (see Acts 7).

Revelation would jump off of the pages I was reading and hearing His voice became much easier. As a result, I began to understand and know God in deeper ways. Because the Holy Spirit loves to testify about Jesus, I began to truly see who Jesus is and what He ultimately came to do.

One of the rolls of the Holy Spirit is contained in Jesus' words found in John 14:26.

> "But the Helper, the Holy Spirit, whom the Father will send in My name, He will teach you all things, and bring to your remembrance all that I said to you."

Because the Holy Spirit teaches us all things and brings to remembrance what Jesus said to us, it was as if the scriptures were breathing. I'd find myself in the midst of a difficult situation and the Holy Spirit would suddenly quote verses to me by flooding my mind with them.

I also began to notice the other amazing ways that God would speak to me in the days that followed my experience. I suddenly realized that God spoke to me in what sounded like my own voice at times or through gentle nudges or knowings. I became aware of spontaneous thoughts I would have that would be reaffirmed in scripture — things I was being urged to do by way of obedience or ideas for the ministry — and I recognized that because I wasn't thinking on those things prior to them occupying my mind, they must have originated with and were from God. In short, I began to be led and guided by the Spirit.

I'd also have dreams from time to time or visions in my mind. Likewise, I also began to see the gift of prophecy manifest through me. I would know certain things about others — things that they were called to do or the different ways God wanted to use them. These phenomenon are also directly correlated to the outpouring of God's Spirit on mankind. They are described as being a byproduct of being baptized in the Holy Spirit and are written about in Acts 2:17-18.

> "'And it shall be in the last days,' God says, 'That I will pour forth of My Spirit on all mankind; And

your sons and your daughters shall prophesy, And your young men shall see visions, And your old men shall dream dreams; Even on My bondslaves, both men and women, I will in those days pour forth of My Spirit and they shall prophesy.'"

We also see prophecy being a manifestation of the baptism in the Holy Spirit when the 12 disciples Paul encounters at Ephesus are filled with the Spirit through the laying on of his hands.

> "And when Paul had laid his hands upon them, the Holy Spirit came on them, and they *began* speaking with tongues and prophesying." (Acts 19:6)

John 16:13 also reaffirms this role of the Spirit in prophecy.

> "But when He, the Spirit of truth, comes, He will guide you into all the truth; for He will not speak on His own initiative, but whatever He hears, He will speak; and He will disclose to you what is to come."

The Holy Spirit speaks to us what He receives from Jesus. He guides us into truth and He is the source behind the gift of prophecy. He is the one who reveals what is to come by His foreknowledge.

GIFTS OF THE SPIRIT

Not only did the gift of prophecy begin to manifest through me, so did such gifts as the word of knowledge, the word of wisdom, the distinguishing or discerning of spirits, and tongues. Never did I see the operation of these gifts in my life prior to being filled with the Spirit. They only appeared once I was baptized in the One who distributes them as He wills (see 1 Corinthians 12:11).

Through the Holy Spirit, the converts in Cornelius' household began speaking in tongues (see Acts 10:46). Through the Holy Spirit, Paul was able to discern the operation of an evil spirit in a young girl (see Acts 16:16-18). Through the Holy Spirit, Agabus prophesied that a famine would occur all over the world (see Acts 11:27-28).

The gifts of the Spirit are by no means merit badges or medals of honor bestowed upon a chosen few. They are tools for the job and they are our inheritance. They aid us in building up and strengthening the church for the common good. Through their operation in our lives, they can also cause someone who has never experienced Jesus before to encounter Him through these manifestations of God's Spirit. If interested, you can read more about this particular ministry of the Spirit in 1 Corinthians 12:4-11.

FINAL REMARKS

There are many wonderful things that take place when you are baptized in the Holy Spirit. In a moment, you can be completely delivered from the sin that so easily entangles you. God becomes undeniably real. You experience the very tangible presence of God in and on your body. You begin to hear God's voice and understand the scriptures. The gifts of the Spirit manifest through you. And the power of God begins to operate in your life.

Before we conclude this section, I want to take a moment to address a doctrine that has done a lot of unintentional damage to people over the years that have sincerely wondered if they are baptized in the Spirit. Although the belief behind this doctrine was never formed to purposefully hurt anyone or polarize or limit this experience, it has caused a lot of people to wonder if they were in fact baptized in the Holy Spirit since they didn't seem to fit the criteria of this doctrine.

The doctrine that I am referring to is the doctrine that adheres to the belief that speaking in tongues is the primary evidence that a person has been filled with the Spirit of God. Although I understand their logic and reasoning for this — having taken Acts 2, the day of Pentecost, as their position — I do not believe that scripture as a whole affirms this position. In fact, the Samaritan believers in Acts 8 received the Holy Spirit through the laying on of hands from Peter and John, but it does not mention that they spoke in tongues.

Personally, it wasn't until a month or so after I was baptized in the Holy Spirit that I began speaking in tongues. Spiritual gifts are something that we are to desire (see 1 Corinthians 14:1) and the gift of tongues is certainly one of those gifts. Even Paul wished that all of the Corinthians spoke in tongues (see 1 Corinthians 14:5). The church at Corinth was a Spirit filled church. That is why Paul had to write to them about the gifts of the Spirit and explain their origin and function within the body of Christ. All appeared to be filled with the Spirit within this church, but not all spoke in tongues.

The reason why the disciples spoke in tongues on the day of Pentecost in Acts 2, in my opinion, was because it was the greatest demonstration of God's power in that particular moment. It was truly a sign and a wonder! There were thousands of people gathered on that day that spoke in various dialects according to their language of origin. God took a group of Galileans and caused them to testify of the mighty works of God in languages they had never spoke in before. The result was amazement and wonder among the hearers and an openness to hear the sermon Peter shared that resulted in their salvation.

Just as I reiterated earlier in this section, I personally believe the initial evidence of being baptized in the Holy Spirit is LOVE. We are commanded to love God and to love others. The whole law and the prophets can be summed up in those two commands. The Holy Spirit gives us this ability through this baptism. He is the One who pours the love of God into our hearts (see Romans 5:5). At the same time, we should earnestly desire spiritual gifts (see 1 Corinthians 14:1).

6

PERSONAL TESTIMONIES

IF GOD DID IT FOR THEM, HE CAN DO IT FOR YOU!

WE'VE ALREADY ESTABLISHED THAT JESUS IS THE ONE who baptizes us in the Holy Spirit. Revelation 19:10 states that the testimony of Jesus is the spirit of prophecy. In other words, individual testimonies declare what Jesus is willing and able to do in the life of the one who hears them. Because God is not a respecter of persons (see Acts 10:34), He is willing to do for you what He did for someone else.

Romans 10:17 declares that faith comes by hearing and hearing by the word of Christ. My hope is that the following testimonies of what Jesus did in the lives of these individuals will produce faith within you to have your own personal encounter with the Holy Spirit. Be encouraged by these real life examples of ordinary people whose lives were forever changed in a moment. Some were healed. Some were delivered. One particular person appears to have been saved and filled with the Spirit at the same time. All was the result of the baptism in the Holy Spirit.

Nearly everyone received it through the laying on of hands. One person, however, received it over the phone! Distance is not a barrier for God! In fact, you'll read about this person's particular encounter in a section all by itself. That's how incredible his story is.

Please note that some of these testimonies were left anonymous at the request of those who received them. It's also important to note that in an effort to preserve the real and raw feel of these testimonies, each story has been presented in the original language and grammar they were written in.

LILY HARE (RED LION AREA SENIOR HIGH SCHOOL STUDENT)

In my Holy Spirit encounter, I received so much revelation pertaining to the kingdom of God, unspeakable joy, and a passion like never before. I experienced a slight shaking sensation and, most of all, an overwhelming sense of peace. It's indescribable what is felt — the loving embrace of the Father, but the most amazing fire from the Holy Spirit. Beautiful, uplifting, encouraging thoughts filled my mind that were straight from the word of God.

I was delivered from the stronghold of a habitual sin that controlled my life more than I thought I could handle. The fruit of my encounter took me into a greater awareness of the presence of God, a heart for evangelism, a deeper understanding of the Lord and how much he desires me. It wrecked me and pushed me into an identity of holiness and purity. It filled me with even more fire for the Lord and a heart for other people to experience the same thing.

Love for the Lord broke through all chains and passion for the gospel completely overcame me and it is evident in my life. People don't always understand me or why I love and seek the Lord so much, but I know that without these encounters I would have never known that the tangible presence of the Lord could be manifested in my daily life. I also learned that you can never have too much of the Holy Spirit. He will fill you again and again and again, as long as you're asking.

SUMMER HARE (RED LION AREA SENIOR HIGH SCHOOL STUDENT)

As I was being prayed over, I felt a tingling through my toes, and it continued to move throughout my body, until, on the 7th prayer, my shoulders were lifted and a difference could clearly be seen. I was sobbing at this point, and even though I'm usually pretty emotional, I felt this pull on my body from God, lifting me from where I had been. My mom even commented on how I looked more "alive," since she can always tell how I feel based on my eyes.

I was healed from a chronic autoimmune issue and was finally able to feel free again! I was having a rough morning beforehand, but after I was filled with the Spirit, everything changed. That's not even an exaggeration - I went from not being able to sit up, to jamming out to music on the car ride back home. Although there are still challenges I face from my autoimmune issue, it's nothing compared to how I felt before the healing.

ANONYMOUS (PRESBYTERIAN CHURCH YOUTH LEADER)

I am 22 years old and am a junior high youth leader in my church's youth group. I have struggled with anxiety for my entire life. I was officially diagnosed when I was 8 years old. It became so debilitating that I couldn't go to school. At that age, I started taking medication. This was not a complete fix, but it took the edge off enough that I could live normally for the most part.

I still had a really hard time going to new places. I also struggled with social anxiety, so I was constantly worried about people looking at me or judging me. In addition to all of that, I still had occasional panic attacks that no medication could ever touch.

I trusted God all along and knew that He had a plan. I prayed for healing, but trusted that if it wasn't God's plan to take it from me, that was okay too. Over the past 8 months, God has begun to heal me. It has been a very slow process, but I had been able to cut my medication dose down to 1/4 of what I was originally taking. The anxiety was still constantly present, but usually bearable.

I was getting ready for the retreat this past weekend and knew God had big plans. I had a really rough day the night before the retreat. I was rear ended in a rental car, which I was driving because my car was in the shop from being rear ended the week before. I also experienced a panic attack, which was very discouraging to me because it had been awhile since I had one. Because of all of this, I was late to the retreat and missed the first session.

The next day, I could feel the Holy Spirit moving so much. I knew God had something huge in store but had no idea what it would look like. Brian began giving testimonies about how God had moved in the past and the Holy Spirit was moving in me so much. He asked anyone who was "feeling it" to come to the front. I went to the front and kept waiting for some crazy awesome vision, or for God to speak to me in some way, but that wasn't happening.

No matter how much I asked God what He wanted to tell me, all I felt was peace. Complete peace. I still had no idea what was going on, and assumed the peace that I was feeling was from being in the presence of the Lord, and not from Him delivering me from my anxiety. I soaked in this peace for a while before God started telling me to pray for specific people around the room. I got up and began to do this, and the peace that I was feeling didn't go anywhere.

You have to understand that my anxiety was a 24/7 thing for the past 14 years. It became easier to deal with when using medication, but it was always there. This peace that I was feeling was different from anything I have ever felt in my entire life. I began to realize that my anxiety was finally gone. I am embarrassed to say that I was still so scared to accept it. I was scared to claim it and then have it come back. I was scared because this has been a part of who I am for as long as I can remember. It seemed way too good to be true. I continued to trust God and I am so excited to say that I have been off of all medications since Sunday, and I have never felt better. GOD IS SO GOOD!

EMILY BRUBAKER (MESSIAH COLLEGE GRADUATE)

The first time I was "filled" I had no idea what it meant. I had no concept for the power of the Holy Spirit, spiritual gifts, or the intimate relationship and encounters you can have with our loving Father. From the baptism of the Holy Spirit that I received from Messiah students that you had taught, I was radically changed in an instant. I met my Maker face to face in the basement of the dorm at Messiah.

From that filling, freedom came. Freedom from guilt, shame, and many sleepless nights. But the greatest was the intimacy that followed. Gods voice became so clear and the fire to pursue Him in every circumstance never left me. The passion to share His love burned like I've never felt. The word became alive and I knew I entered into a deeper relationship than I have ever known before. It never stopped from that moment.

I knew God would relentlessly pursue me forever and the Holy Spirit would move in power in ways I never expected. In the following days I saw people healed, demons flee, emotional bondages had no place, prophetic words were spoken, and tongues flow all from my hands and mouth. The girl who never knew what those words meant was experiencing the power and love of God from that wonderful infilling.

STEVE GOSS (CO-FOUNDER OF THE FOUNDRY—BRIDGEVILLE, DE)

I believe it was the fall of 2012 when you came the first time to Gateway Fellowship. I was finally getting used to living in Delaware. I had spent the previous 3 years fighting God on being there. I was wanting to move back home to Illinois and hated everyone who said that I should be in Delaware.

Eventually, I made my peace with God on the matter and He was starting to reveal more and more of His heart to me when you came. I remember thinking that the message you brought was like a stick of dynamite thrown into my perception of God as Father and myself as a son.

I had always known these things from growing up in church, but now God was making them real to me. My identity and destiny were awakened. I don't think I had ever experienced true hunger or even knew what that was, but now I found myself starving for more of God. He started speaking to me in ways I had never heard before.

The Spirit fell that weekend in a mighty way. I went from being filled with uncontrollable laughter to being laid out on the floor for hours to speaking in tongues for the first time. This was all new to me. I had never experienced anything like this and in fact I had been critical of those who said they had been slain in the spirit. I wrote them off as 'fakers,' but this was definitely real.

God forever changed me that weekend. I found myself praying for the sick at work (which I never would have done before) and to my surprise they were being healed. He set a heart of worship in me and gave me fresh vision and dreams for my musical talents, but most of all, He awakened my identity and showed me that He wasn't an angry father waiting to punish me for my failures. Rather, He was a loving Daddy who just wants to love on me and for the first time I felt God's joy and pride to call me son.

ANONYMOUS (UNIVERSITY OF PITTSBURGH JOHNSTOWN GRADUATE)

I was raised a Lutheran, but I never had an intimate

relationship with Christ. I started going to my friend's youth group in 2012, and from that summer, my relationship with Him became a stronger part of my life. But I was also struggling with anorexia and the feelings of insecurity would never go away no matter how much I tried. I'd look in the mirror and just cry because of how much I hated myself. Even though I did get thin, I was never skin and bones, the image that comes to most minds when they think of the word "anorexia," but it was still a problem.

I enjoyed feeling hungry and felt better about myself when I did not eat. This was always a part of my life that I felt so guilty about because I should not have been doing that to myself. I knew God was hurt when I did.

Fast forward to 2014. It was the middle of my first year at Pitt-Johnstown and I attended a worship service at the chapel when Pastor Brian came as a visitor to speak. God really had His hand on me that night because my life was transformed. Brian prayed for me to be filled with the Spirit and I felt this outrageous tingle in the core of my stomach. It was a feeling I'll never forget. I can't explain it.

The feeling extended through my body to the tips of my fingers and I lost all control of my body and fell to the ground. Something in me changed, and I didn't hate myself anymore. I realized that Christ loves me, and that is enough for me to love myself. The bad that I thought about myself literally made its way out of me and all of a sudden, I felt so changed because of the love of God, all in that instant.

GAVIN SMITH (STUDENT)

I just wanted to start off by saying thank you. You brought so much healing and love when you called the Holy Spirit to fill the room. My best friend who has never cried in his life did that night. My best friends that are girls were overcome with joy. I felt tingles, I was swaying, I was able to play songs in my head and tap them out on my leg. The Holy Spirit took away a lot of pain that I had in my life.

I suffered from rejection after rejection from girls because I was searching for love apart from the love provided by my family. So from there, I became addicted to pornography. I felt if I couldn't find love anywhere else, then I could find it there. I went through the exact pain you went through. Passwords, restrictions, etc. My parents found out and restricted me from everything. But the restrictions didn't hold me back. I found a way. But last night I was released of the pain and lust. It was glorious.

ALLISON WHING (UPSTREAM FAMILY MINISTRIES)

When the Holy Spirit first began to fall at my church, I wasn't sure what to think. There was nothing in my upbringing that gave me any kind of understanding. I thought manifestations were weird and I didn't think they were even real.

The first service I went to where the Spirit was falling kinda freaked me out. I wasn't sure what to think or how to handle it. But I watched and took it all in. There was something that stirred in me and wanted to know if it was real but I was also afraid — afraid it wasn't real, afraid it was real, afraid of what I would look like if I manifested Him.

The second service I went to, Pastor Brian spoke about the spirit of fear. I had never heard of fear as a spirit and everything he said made so much sense. When I went to the front for prayer, that's what I asked for, that the spirit of fear would be released. When he prayed for me, I didn't feel anything leave, but when he was done, I kind of felt light, as though something was lifted but I couldn't describe it.

I wandered around the people who were laying around and went to the front. My husband was there and so I thought maybe he was experiencing something and we could be together. Someone came up behind me and lightly placed their hands on me. I could hear them speaking in tongues but I didn't know who it was.

All of a sudden, I felt heat rising up my legs and they started to feel like jelly. I felt myself being pulled back towards the floor like a magnet. I had no control over my body. My eyes were closed and I found myself holding onto this person and sobbing out of control. In the moment I didn't understand what had happened but it felt like I was crying and spitting. It probably only lasted less than a minute but suddenly it was all over and I looked up.

Thankfully I was holding onto a friend (it was she who had laid hands on me and prayed in tongues). I was like, "What happened?" Stuff was coming out of my mouth and I had no control over it and I didn't know how to stop it but couldn't try if I wanted to. I then realized I had been speaking in tongues.

The rest of the day, I kind of felt like I was in a haze. My brain was kind of fuzzy. I slept normally that night and then the next day got up for work like I normally do. I hadn't prepared lunch for the day so I stopped at the grocery store.

I pulled into the parking lot and turned up the music. I opened my mouth to sing but instead of words, tongues started flowing from my mouth again. I literally couldn't stop them. I was driving and looking around the parking lot for a parking space, tongues flowing, me with my eyes wide not understanding what was happening. I parked the car and suddenly the tongues stopped without warning. And then I burst out laughing. Gut wrenching laughing. I thought about how ridiculous it all was which made me laugh even harder.

I had to get out of the car and get lunch or I'd be late to work so I went into the store and I was literally skipping. I couldn't stop my body. If I opened my mouth, I would start speaking in tongues. I was basically muttering in tongues under my breath. I got into the car and called my pastor on the way to work. He told me to just go with it.

I worked in public school, but not in a classroom, so, thankfully, I had a small office. The entire day, I was speaking in tongues. They just kept coming out of nowhere and I couldn't stop them. I tried to stay in my office all day because when I would talk to someone, tongues and giggles would come out. I felt literally drunk until the afternoon when it subsided.

After this experience of being baptized in the Spirit, I was able to hear more clearly from the Lord. I felt Him asking hard things of me and while it took my faith a long time to catch up, I knew it was from Him. I also felt He gave me dreams in that season which took many years for me to pursue, but I link all of it back to that season. I wish I had been more obedient directly in the moment.

I also know that I've been given the gift of tongues. I've seen some miraculous things that happened as a result of using tongues to pray over people. I don't always understand this gift and it was the one that I never wanted because to me, it was too weird. But it's given me a level of freedom I never had before. When I don't know what or how to pray, I'll pray in tongues. Sometimes it will suddenly come over me and I have to just pray and get it out. I've even prayed in tongues in my dreams against things. I strongly believe that I had to have the spirit of fear off of me in order to receive the baptism of the Spirit. For me, it came immediately after Pastor Brian prayed for it to go.

ADAM BOWER (LEAD PASTOR, PRAISE COMMUNITY CHURCH)

Brian was in my kitchen and he was sharing about his experience with being filled with the Holy Spirit. I was skeptical because of all of the negativity that surrounds charismatic sensationalism. He was my best friend, so I knew he wasn't lying, and he seemed so sincere. I asked him if he thought the Holy Spirit would do for me what He did for him. He said, "I don't know, but we can pray and find out."

He laid one hand on my upper back and he began to pray. Roughly 90 seconds went by, but it felt like an eternity. I went to turn around to thank him for praying, but when I went to do so, I couldn't move. Suddenly, it felt like I was being pulled to the floor. It was as if the weight of gravity increased ten times its amount.

The last thought I remember having in the chair was this: "Oh my God. I am going to smack my head off the floor." I went down like a sack of potatoes. While I laid on the floor, I went back and forth between laughing hysterically and sobbing uncontrollably. The emotions were so intense as they came at what seemed like intervals of two minutes back and forth. When I came to, my yellow lab was licking my face. I don't know how long I was on the floor, but I had a puddle of drool, tears, and snot beneath me.

I was wobbly getting up. I felt drunk and could barely get around. I was still laughing and crying, but now I was leaning against walls trying to function normally. The experience of feeling drugged lasted probably for 6 hours, only calming down as the day moved on.

I was delivered from three things that day. The fear of man and caring about what people thought was gone. The fear that was present in my marriage was ripped out. I had an underlying feeling that my wife was going to leave me, but that was a lie from the enemy. Third, my relationship with my Dad was restored in my heart, and all the bitterness was removed, and the enemy's seed was exposed and dealt with.

Finally, I believed what the Bible said in a more significant way. Faith increased to the point that I was praying for others with such expectation and watching God move in an incredible direction.

MATTHEW YOST (6TH GRADE STUDENT)

"I'm really nervous," I thought to myself. I sat still on my chair as the clapping and cheering started to die down. "I have no idea what will happen tonight," I thought. No single clue.

Pastor Brian came onto the stage. He begins to speak. He starts to get into what he was going to teach all of us that night, when all of a sudden, I start to feel a tightness in my stomach. It wasn't an afraid or scared tightness. It was something different. But I couldn't pick it out.

I knew it was something big. It almost felt like butterflies in my stomach. But it wasn't like the nervous kind, even though I was really nervous.

I was feeling really, really nervous now. Pastor Brian kept on speaking when I started to feel it even more. It was starting to rise up into my throat and it was even stronger.

At that moment, I got up, walked to the front and knelt down. I sat down on the carpeted floor and started to pray. "Yes!" I thought, "I will finally get to have a testimony!"

Right then, everything that I was feeling left. I couldn't feel it anymore. I was confused. It was there, but now it wasn't.

"What?" I thought, "What happened?" I wanted Jesus to come into my heart. So that is what I said to Him. "I want you to come into my heart," I whispered and I kept repeating it. And when I did that, all the nerves left. And I knew they were gone for good. I knew God was in the room and I knew that He was right there, right where I was sitting.

Pastor Brian stopped and started to pray over us. I listened to what he was saying, but I was also saying my own tiny prayer in my head. Then, all of a sudden, a voice came into my head. "I am who I always was. I love you and I will be with you wherever you go." And that just made me burst into tears.

I fell down all the way to the ground. More tears came streaming down my face. It felt like the whole world just got flipped upside down, and I couldn't control it. More and more tears came streaming down my face because I didn't know someone in that high of a position could actually love me the way He does.

I knew it was God's voice, even if it wasn't loud and booming. I felt so sorry for all those years that I shut Him out. I never ever wanted to do that again. I didn't even know why He still cared.

Then, I realized why I didn't have that type of encounter at the other encounter nights. It took me back to when I read this one verse in the bible. "If you seek Me with all your heart you will find Me" — Jeremiah 29:13. I didn't have that kind of encounter because I wasn't seeking Him with all my heart and this time I was.

JOANNA MULL (MESSIAH COLLEGE GRADUATE)

Prior to my encounter with the Holy Spirit, I wasn't sure what being a follower of Jesus was about. I never understood why people would willingly choose to follow the rules in the Bible if they didn't have to. Though I was raised in a Christian household and attended church, Sunday school, youth group, etc., I never had the desire to adhere to what I was being taught; I did so begrudgingly. I believed in God, but could not develop a relationship and lacked the drive to pursue Him.

When I was 14, I first fell victim to demonic powers. After falling asleep one night, demons spoke to me. I was aware of what was going on around me – technically awake – but found that my body was paralyzed; therefore, I could not "wake up" (a traumatic experience called Sleep Paralysis). The voices taunted me, laughed at me, and I was powerless to stop it. From that point on, demons would regularly visit me while I slept.

I was always the kid growing up who slept with a night light on, but once these visits began, my fear of the dark was debilitating. My waking hours were spent dreading night time. Bedtime meant heart-racing, fist-clenching fear. Luckily I shared a room with my sister – which helped the fear somewhat. When she was gone, I stayed awake all night, too scared to sleep. I dreaded waking up in the middle of the night to go to the bathroom; the walk from my bed to the light switch that illuminated the hallway was terrifying. I could feel an evil presence all around me; the hair on my arms and neck would stand straight up.

Fast forward 8 years to January of my senior year of college. I began to fear what life after school would look like. Would my living situation always include a roommate with whom I shared a bedroom? If not, how would I cope as an adult living with this paralyzing fear of nighttime and the dark?

While these concerns swirled in my head, I also began to feel freshly confused about what I lacked spiritually that caused my Christ-honoring friends to walk their narrow path with lightness, humility, and joy. For the first time, I started to feel hungry for something I knew I was missing.

On a cold night in February, my roommate came back to our shared apartment and told me that I needed to attend a Bible study that she had just attended. I could tell that whatever had been taught at this study had impacted her greatly. Her face was shining and she could barely contain her excitement. I waited prayerfully in anticipation all week. Somehow, I knew that there was something in store for me through this Bible study.

On February 13th, I went with a few friends and sat in a small classroom on our college campus. Truthfully, I never really particularly enjoyed listening to sermons or Bible studies, but I remember being shocked when

Brian took a short break from speaking and I realized that 2 hours had passed. His words were filled with scripture references, and he spoke with power and confidence.

When we came back from our short bathroom break, my hands were shaking and I felt chills all through my body. Brian quietly said, "I'm going to invite the Holy Spirit to come now. If you want, you can put your hands up in a gesture of receiving." I did so.

Brian began to pray and clapped his hands once. As soon as he clapped, I instantly felt an indescribable surge through my body. I knew right away that something supernatural was occurring. My whole body was shaking and I realized I was half crying and half laughing. Around me, I saw students experiencing the Holy Spirit. I got up and walked toward Brian. My legs were wobbly and I could barely stand up straight. He prayed over me and my legs gave out. Thankfully, someone was there to catch me!

I experienced sudden clarity and knew that I had to tell someone about my struggles with sleep. Tanya, a woman from Brian's church who had joined him, was standing nearby, and I got up and shakily walked over to her. I could barely speak, but I remember getting out,

"Demons talk to me in my sleep. I haven't slept in 8 years."

Without asking any questions, Tanya laid hands on me and began to pray. In Jesus' name, she rebuked the devil. I started coughing and remember feeling embarrassed that I was ruining a prayer that was being offered up on my behalf!

Tanya continued to pray and suddenly my cough became strong enough that my legs gave out and I fell to the floor. Tanya helped break my fall. As I was laying on the ground, she whispered prayers for peace in Jesus' name. All of a sudden, my shuddering, shaking body became completely still. Though people around me were crying, praying out loud, laughing, rejoicing, I felt so at peace that I could have fallen asleep.

My life did a complete 180 after that night. My sleep was deep, sweet, refreshing. I did not fear the night. The demons that had taken hold of my fear had fled at the name of Jesus. Though prior to being baptized in the Spirit, I would tell myself over and over again, "God is protecting me, God is watching out for me." Now, I finally believed it and acknowledged the truth written in Psalm 91, knowing that darkness is as light to the Lord.

Not only was I finally able to sleep in peace, but scripture came alive to me! I remember being enthralled with the Gospels. I can recall spending hours pouring over passages, making notes and highlighting truths I was realizing for the first time.

Worship changed. Not only was I newly engaged in the physical act of musical worship – I had always rolled my eyes at people who raised their hands – I began to realize that worship was more than just music time on Sunday morning. It was a way of honoring God in every aspect of my life.

I prayed for those who irritated me, because my heart felt soft. My level of humility and ability to apologize for my wrongdoing suddenly...existed. I believed with my whole heart in the Holy Spirit's ability to heal the sick and the wounded and witnessed and took part in many supernatural encounters where hands were laid and prayers were offered in the name of Jesus.

I was able to recognize that the Spirit is communicating with me all the time, if I listen for Him. By relying on the Spirit, I've been blessed with visions, peace during trials, and the right words to suddenly flow out of me when I didn't know what to say. Prayer became a powerful tool. I had experienced the God who HEARS my prayers in a tangible way.

Because of the dramatic and supernatural nature of my

encounter, I knew without a doubt that God was good and does good. Even now, in the midst of trial or a tragic death, I remember that act of healing and it draws my focus to the linear, unending goodness of my Creator.

The biggest change that came as a result of my encounter with the Holy Spirit is the desire in my heart to love Jesus and to serve Him above everything else. 1 John 5:3 perfectly reflects my transformation: "For this is the love of God, that we keep His commandments; and His commandments are not burdensome." This desire has changed the whole trajectory of my life. God continues to challenge and grow me, but my heart continues to seek after serving the Lord and growing His kingdom.

7
HEALING JAPAN

BAPTIZED IN THE SPIRIT OVER THE PHONE

The following testimony is from an ordinary man who felt called to move to Japan to share the gospel. While there, he became increasingly aware that something was missing from his Christian witness. It was the feeling of this void that caused him to search for an answer. As a result, his search led him to a book. The book led him to the author. And the author led him to the One who changed this man's life and witness forever.

It was through just one prayer over the phone that this man received the power to perform what you are about to read through his story. To be honest, this testimony both challenges and humbles me. I'm humbled to have played a role in this man's life, but I'm also convicted by his example. My hope and prayer is that you, too, will be provoked to seek out and walk in the power that clothed my dear friend.

JEFF PACK

In 2010, I was living in Los Angeles, California. God told me to go to Japan. I knew it was a word from Him. I got a job as an English teacher to pay my way there and began working in a classroom full time teaching English. My ministry was that I would invite students from my class that I had good rapport with to a weekly God meeting I had at the library on the third floor where you could talk out loud. We would read the Bible and talk about God. I hung out with these people as they were my friends and they grew eager to read God's word with me.

Fast forward to 2012 where I had been in Japan for 18 months. A friend of mine told me their grandfather had been diagnosed with cancer. I hopped on the bullet train and road several hours back to the city I had lived in my first year in Japan. We went to the library and got a bilingual Bible and I told my friend to read to her grandfather Acts chapter 3 because a man in there had been miraculously healed.

Her grandfather sat in his bed and gave us his full attention. He was receiving this with open arms. That's all I did because I didn't know anything else to do. He died.

I went back to Tokyo so upset. I thought that this could never happen again. I went in my room and fasted and prayed for 3 weeks. I only came out of my room to teach an English lesson and then I went back to seeking God in my room.

I contacted a pastor in the US and asked if I needed to be baptized with the Holy Spirit. He said, "No. You got that when you believed in Jesus." I went back to seeking the Lord.

After about about two weeks, God told me to type something in Amazon and when I did, a book came up from an author I had never heard of, but I knew God wanted me to read this book. It was called, "First Dance: Venturing Deeper Into a Relationship with God" by Brian Connolly. I read it immediately and swallowed it right up.

I was left thinking to myself, "I have to have what this guy is talking about in this book." I started searching online for the author. I found he was a pastor at a church and got his email from the church website. I emailed him and told him about this and asked if I could please talk to him, that I wanted what he talked about in this book. He generously agreed and we scheduled a time.

At the exact time we scheduled, I called him on his cell phone. He was in Pennsylvania and I was in Tokyo, Japan. He answered the phone so calmly and said he was just sipping on his coffee waiting for my call. Then the first thing he said to me after that was, "Have you been baptized in the Holy Spirit?" I said, "No."

I didn't say this to him, but I didn't know anything about that. I hadn't even heard of it before. He said, "I am going to pray for you and at some point I will get off the phone but you stay in that place." I said, "Ok."

He started to pray and I felt prompted to lie down. So I was lying on my little mat that I slept on in my studio apartment in Tokyo while this man I never met prayed for me. I have no idea what he prayed. All I know is that my feet started to come off the ground. I kid you not... I was like, "What in the world is happening?"

Then he kept praying. I think he said the word "more" but I'm not sure. Then my upper body came off the ground. I was now sitting on my butt and nothing else was touching the ground. My stomach got so tight —

just like I was doing a hard crunch exercise. Then, my body started doing involuntary crunches really hard.

I would be lying flat on my back and then my whole body would crunch really hard together leaving only my butt on the ground. This went on and on and eventually, Brian left the call. I stopped all of this and as I laid flat on the ground, I wondered if this was me doing this. So I decided to be completely limp to make sure it wasn't me.

As soon as I decided this, I started doing intense crunches all over again. It was so intense inside my belly — harder than any crunch I had ever done. From the time Brian prayed until this physical intensity ended was 55 minutes. I checked the clock as soon as I got up from this. My forehead was sweating. I wondered what had just happened.

The next evening I lied down on the mat again. I had done a lot of comedy and acting earlier in my life and laughter was really important to me. I was voted class clown with my buddy in high school. I asked God if we could do this again like the night before but this time for it to be about laughter. As soon as I said that to God, I started laughing. This joy and laughter came on me and this went on for a while just like the night before, except, it was just this really hilarious laughter. I knew something had happened.

That week I was walking from a cafe down the sidewalk in Tokyo and my stomach started doing those crunches while I was walking around. Right around the time of this week, I started getting this download in my head. It was a revelation that we could lay hands on the sick and they would recover. Keep in mind that I didn't know anything about this, didn't know anyone who knew anything about this, and I was by myself in Japan. God started showing me His word and preachers that talked about this. I remember Matthew 10 and Mark 16 very specifically. I realized that God was telling me to heal the sick.

When I was in West Hollywood in my apartment before I left for Japan, God told me that the word for my time in Japan was called, "Healing Japan." I started a blog called Healing Japan in 2010. Campus Crusade and Faith Comes by Hearing partnered with me.

I received resources from Campus Crusade to help me. They gave me comic books in Japanese with the Jesus story in them, which I gave to my students because they didn't look like anything but a comic book. The school manager saw one and just thought it was a comic book, which was exactly what the intention was of keeping it hidden.

Faith Comes by Hearing helped me get the Japanese audio Bible on my blog and those two groups helped me get the Jesus film in Japanese on my blog as well. I had no idea why God told me the word, "Healing Japan." I just thought I was going to share about Jesus and that hearts would be healed in terms of getting saved. I didn't know this meant that I would literally be healing people.

Once God gave me this revelation and understanding, I immediately set out to do it. I mean within just a few days or a week of Brian praying for me, I was walking to the school in central Tokyo to teach an English lesson and on my way I saw a man with an arm brace on both arms to aid him with his walking. I asked if I could pray for him. He said, "No." I said, "Please. I really want to!" He said, "No."

I got to class and while teaching my lesson, a student walked in late on crutches. She hadn't been on crutches before. After class when everyone was packing up their stuff, I went up to her. A couple people were around her desk as well and I asked her what happened. She said she injured her foot the night before. I think she said it was from gymnastics.

I asked if I could pray for her foot and she said yes. I put my hand on her foot and said, "Be healed in Jesus' name." I asked her how it was, if it was better. She said, "No." She said her foot was painful. I prayed again.

Keep in mind I had never seen anyone or known anyone to pray for a sick person like this. The second time I asked her she said it wasn't healed. It was the same. I prayed again. I just said, "In Jesus' name, be healed." I didn't close my eyes or talk to God. I just put my hands on her foot and said what I said because of Mark 16:17-18.

After the third time, she was wide eyed like a deer in headlights. She intensely said, "What did you do?!" Her foot was instantly healed. I said, "It was Jesus." She asked me again. Three times she asked me and my answer was Jesus. She didn't know that name so I told her the name in Japanese and she said, "Oh." The next class she came back with no crutches. I realized this was real. I started to pursue this healing.

Before Brian prayed for me, my ministry in Japan was inviting people I knew well to a Bible study and tried to lead them to believe in Jesus through His word. It worked, but it wasn't exciting. After Brian prayed for me, I became so bold. I was walking up to people on the street now. I didn't do that before in this way. I was studying healing now in my room and going up to a minimum of 12 people on the street a day. I was being screamed at in my face to get away and it didn't phase me at all.

In Fukuyama, Hiroshima, I saw a man in a wheelchair at the library. I asked to pray for him and after I did I said, "Now get up and walk." He looked at me like I had lost my mind and I told him I was serious. "Now get up," I said. He got up and walked. He just had a small limp but he walked.

Then, in Tokyo, I saw a man in a wheelchair as I went down a small side street outside some shops. I stopped and talked with him. He was elderly. I asked to pray for him and told him to get up out of the wheelchair. When I did, he stood up, but his back was bent over 90 degrees like he was still in the chair. I went behind him and asked him to stand up. He said he couldn't go any further because of his back. I put my hands on his back and said, "Be healed in Jesus' name. Stand up."

He stood straight up. I got his phone number to plug him into someone local and he literally walked off pushing his wheelchair. He was completely healed and turned around to wave at me as he walked off. I was so pumped it was ridiculous!

I searched for anyone I could find in Japan with this

faith. I found one person. A young man who had studied at John G Lake Ministries in Texas and had translated their Divine Healing Technician book into Japanese. We met at a cafe. I invited him to go pray for people with me. He said that he could not believe that I wasn't trained by anyone and that everything that I was doing and saying was like what he had been trained to do and say, but more powerful and with deeper insight. All I knew was that when Brian prayed for me something changed. It was the Holy Spirit. Not me.

We went together to a market place in Tokyo to pray for every sick person that passed by. We sort of got split up and I approached a man who looked sick. He was a stocky fellow. I asked him if I could pray for him and he punched me, knocking me straight to the ground. After I got my breath back, I got up and walked straight up to him again and very gently asked if I could pray for him. He looked at me wide eyed. He didn't know what to do. I hadn't changed my disposition at all towards him. He didn't say a word. He turned and walked away.

I was unmoved by the encounter but my stomach really hurt from where he punched me. I told my friend and he was surprised that had happened. I laid hands on my belly and it was healed within a few moments. I looked over and there was a group of people with down syndrome. I approached the leader and asked to pray for them. She gave me the green light and I called my friend over. We laid hands on each one of them individually.

He was bilingual in English and Japanese while I could barely speak enough Japanese to function. He asked me to go to a man's house who was terminally ill. He translated everything for me. This encounter was incredible! The man was healed of so many things that this testimony alone would be a book, but a couple highlights are that I got a word about his artery being clogged and he confirmed it was true.

I never heard of "words" before. It just happened. Also, he couldn't walk without a big wooden walking cane. The doorbell rang while we were ministering to him and when he got back from checking the door I asked him if he realized that he had walked to the door with no cane. He didn't know that he had just done that. He was healed. He told us he had one arm shorter than another and I told him that we didn't need to pray for that. It was already healed. He straightened his arms in front of him to check and they were perfectly even. His eyes opened wide and the interpreter started laughing at his expression.

There are so many testimonies from healing in Japan that have come out of this baptism in the Holy Spirit. The interpreter had one leg shorter and when I prayed for it, it grew out to be the same length as the other leg. He had a disease where he was bald in the middle of his head at only 26 years old. The doctors couldn't help him. I prayed for his head and laid hands on it in a restaurant. After that, his hair grew back in the exact opposite way as one loses their hair naturally. It grew in thin and grey and then thicker and then grew in towards the center and became dark black like the rest of his head. He wore hats to cover it from embarrassment and I'd say within three months or so of laying my hand on his head, it was completely made whole.

After Japan, God led me to move to Santa Monica, CA. I did marketing in a real estate office. There were so many healings in that office it was just ridiculous. One of the top earners there walked in one day hunched over. He had pulled his back out and he was limping. I went into his office and shut the door. I prayed for him a couple times and he stood straight up and was instantly healed. He immediately said he wanted to open a healing room in the office.

Healing isn't the only thing that flowed after Brian prayed for me. It's just one aspect I want to share. Dreams, words of knowledge, tongues... so many things. But the biggest change of all was a download of the Father's love. I was sitting in my room in Tokyo around the time Brian prayed for me (within a week I'd say) and just realizing how much love the Father was pouring out. I started going around giving people chocolate and telling them how Jesus loved them. My love for people grew much more deep after the Holy Spirit made his home in me.

Today, I am in fellowship with the Holy Spirit. I have a relationship with him as a person. I love Him so much. I talk to him when I wake up. He goes with me everywhere and He makes himself known.

I didn't know about the Holy Spirit baptism before Brian prayed for me and my life has not been the same since. I am eternally grateful for the time he generously gave me. How bold is it of Brian to pray for me on the phone from a different country that God would show up and make his home inside of me. Come on!

I write all this to say that I wasn't getting much accomplished without the Holy Spirit. But with Him, the kingdom of God is forcefully advancing wherever I go and my relationship with God is so precious.

8

HOW CAN I RECEIVE THE BAPTISM IN THE HOLY SPIRIT?

BELIEVE

The first thing you have to do is believe that this experience is just as much for today as it was on the day of Pentecost. It's imperative that you understand that the one who baptizes in the Holy Spirit, Jesus Christ, never changes. And it's important that you trust that He can and wants to fill you with the Holy Spirit. It's faith that causes us to position ourselves to receive what we believe.

HUNGER AND THIRST

The greatest thing you'll ever possess in this life is your

personal hunger for God. The bible calls those blessed who hunger and thirst for righteousness (see Matthew 5:6). It also says that these same people will be satisfied. Therefore, if you hunger to receive the baptism in the Holy Spirit, it will be yours. Hunger is like a spiritual ATM card. It makes a withdrawal on the Spirit of God. It draws Him to you.

In John 7:37-39, Jesus also invites those who thirst for more of God to come to Him.

> "If anyone is thirsty, let him come to Me and drink. He who believes in Me, as the Scripture said, 'From his innermost being will flow rivers of living water.'" But this He spoke of the Spirit, whom those who believed in Him were to receive; for the Spirit was not yet *given*, because Jesus was not yet glorified."

There is nothing casual about being hungry and thirsty. They are intense, physical feelings and they can feel just as intense on a spiritual level. To be hungry and thirsty is to be overcome with desire for the only thing that can satiate those cravings. Hunger and thirst does not cross its arms and think, "Well, if it happens, it happens."

NO!

The thirsty person will continue to come to Jesus until they receive the drink He has promised to give. This drink is the Holy Spirit. It's God Himself.

It's wonderful that Jesus makes it so simple. Do you thirst? Then you will be satisfied!

If you don't find yourself hungry and thirsty for God, ask Him to make you so! Read the testimonies of those who have received the baptism in the Spirit. Ask people to tell you their stories about when they received it and what happened as a result. Read the book of Acts in its entirety. It will be like salt in your mouth. They will make you thirsty to be filled with the Spirit of God!

ASK

The baptism in the Holy Spirit is called the gift of God (see Acts 2:38). It is something that we can ask for. Take a look at what Luke 11:9-13 has to say.

> "So I say to you, ask, and it will be given to you; seek, and you will find; knock, and it will be opened to you. For everyone who asks, receives; and he who seeks, finds; and to him who knocks, it will be

opened. Now suppose one of you fathers is asked by his son for a fish; he will not give him a snake instead of a fish, will he? Or *if* he is asked for an egg, he will not give him a scorpion, will he? If you then, being evil, know how to give good gifts to your children, how much more will *your* heavenly Father give the Holy Spirit to those who ask Him?"

Your Father in heaven is a kind and generous father. No good thing does He withhold from those who ask. Hebrews 11:6 tells us that He is the rewarder of those who seek Him. I can promise you that it greatly pleases the Father when we ask Him in faith for what it is that He has promised to give. He loves to be wanted. This is why He is willing and eager to baptize His people with His Spirit and to do it again and again.

PERSIST

Perseverance is the greatest demonstration of faith. In the face of waiting to receive what its heart is set on, it declares, "I'm not wavering. I know what's been promised to me, and I will continue to ask, seek, and knock until it's mine." Sadly, it's the waiting that causes many people to shipwreck and throw in the towel. But the evidence that we truly believe is that we continue to position ourselves to receive what we are waiting for.

Jesus' parable in Luke 11:5-8 reinforces this idea.

> "Then He said to them, 'Suppose one of you has a friend, and goes to him at midnight and says to him, 'Friend, lend me three loaves; for a friend of mine has come to me from a journey, and I have nothing to set before him'; and from inside he answers and says, 'Do not bother me; the door has already been shut and my children and I are in bed; I cannot get up and give you *anything*.' I tell you, even though he will not get up and give him *anything* because he is his friend, yet because of his persistence he will get up and give him as much as he needs."

After His resurrection, Jesus appeared to 500 people (see 1 Corinthians 15:6). Why is it that there were only 120 gathered in the upper room on the day of Pentecost? Could it be that not everyone is willing to wait for what God has promised? Those that waited and received what was promised changed history forever. They persevered. We are believers today because of their willingness to spread the gospel!

PRAY

One of the ways that we persist is through our constant

asking, seeking, and knocking in prayer. We noticed that the disciples were filled with the Holy Spirit while waiting on God in prayer in Acts 2 and 4. One of my good friends received this experience when His hunger and thirst caused him to get alone and wait until the Spirit filled him with His glorious presence. In an effort to simulate and encourage what he felt was a holy moment, he lit a candle, went into a dark room, and sat silently until the Lord baptized him.

THE LAYING ON OF HANDS

Another way to receive the baptism in the Holy Spirit is through the laying on of hands by those that have already been filled with the Holy Spirit. The laying on of hands was considered to be an elementary teaching of the church (see Hebrews 6:2). It was used for blessing, commissioning, healing, and impartation (the transference of the anointing of the Spirit from one person to another).

In Acts 8 and 19, both Peter and John laid hands on the new converts in Samaria while Paul laid his hands on the new converts he encountered in Ephesus. Immediately, they were filled with the Holy Spirit. I'm a firm advocate of encouraging those who wish to be baptized with the Spirit to attend meetings and conferences where this ministry is being taught and practiced. Keep going to such places until you receive what you are thirsting for! You can also ask anyone who has been baptized in the Spirit to lay hands on you and pray for you to receive the same experience.

9
PRAYER OF IMPARTATION

IN ROMANS 1:11, PAUL TOLD THE CHURCH IN ROME THAT he longed to see them and impart some spiritual gift to them. Similarly, I desire that you, too, would receive an impartation; namely, that the anointing that I've received through the baptism in the Holy Spirit would be given to you. If Jesus can baptize my friend, Jeff, with the Holy Spirit over the phone, He can baptize you while reading what you are about to read.

For that reason, I offer this prayer on your behalf. I pray that through your reading it, you will receive a most glorious experience. I pray that you would be bountifully filled with the Spirit of God and that all that you have read about in this book will begin to manifest in your life!

Heavenly Father, I thank you for the promise of the baptism in the Holy Spirit through Jesus Christ. I'm grateful that He is the same today, yesterday, and forever. I'm thankful for impartation — the transference of the anointing of the Holy Spirit from one person's life to another's. I pray for every person reading this book that they would be baptized in the Holy Spirit.

Come, Holy Spirit...

Holy Spirit, I pray that you would come to the person holding this book right now. I pray that You would come and fill them with Yourself. I pray that they would be forever changed. I pray that that they'd be set free of any bondage. I pray that You would become undeniably real. I pray that You would do for them what it is that You did for me.

Bless them, Father. Make them hungrier than they've ever been. Make them thirstier than they've ever been. And may their lives be marked with encounters with You this day forward.

In Jesus' name I pray.

Amen.

ABOUT THE AUTHOR

Brian has been involved in full time ministry since 2005. He has served as both a youth pastor and teaching pastor within the local church and stepped out into full time itinerant ministry in 2019. It was at this time that he founded Faith Like Birds Ministries.

As an itinerant minister, Brian travels both nationally and internationally and ministers at conferences, home groups, youth groups, and churches. He loves to share what he believes God is saying to those he ministers to and to see people encounter God in a way that brings transformation. He is also very passionate about wanting to see the next generation experience God in a way that makes Him undeniably real.

Brian is the author of two other books, First Dance: Venturing Deeper Into a Relationship with God and Awakened: Coming Awake and Coming Alive Through the Beauty of the Gospel. He is also the creator and director of The Unveiling Prophetic School, a two year school that equips students in the fundamentals of the gift of prophecy and in understanding their identity as believers. He is also the founder of The Shout Crusades, large sized evangelistic meetings for youth to encounter God and be set free.

Brian is a graduate of Asbury Theological Seminary in Wilmore, KY and Millersville University in Lancaster, PA. He possesses an MA in Counseling and a BA in English, with a minor in Psychology.

Brian also has a large family that consists of his wife, Nicole, and his four girls, Emma, Lily, Hannah, and Shiloh, and his Rottweiler, Maximus.

For more information about Brian and his ministry, or if you are interested in inviting Brian to minister, connect online at:

FaithLikeBirds.com

Made in the USA
Middletown, DE
09 April 2021